CATS

PERSIAN CATS

STUART A. KALLEN

ABDO & Daughters

Published by Abdo & Daughters, 4940 Viking Drive, Suite 622, Edina, Minnesota 55435.

Library bound edition distributed by Rockbottom Books, Pentagon Tower, P.O. Box 36036, Minneapolis, Minnesota 55435.

Printed in the United States.

Cover Photo credit: Peter Arnold, Inc.

Interior Photo credits: Peter Arnold, Inc.

Edited by Rosemary Wallner

Library of Congress Cataloging-in-Publication Data

Kallen, Stuart A., 1955   Persian cat / by Stuart A. Kallen.
         p. cm. — (Cats)
Includes bibliographical references (p. 24) and index.
ISBN 1-56239-445-2
1. Persian cat—Juvenile literature. [1. Persian cat. 2. Cats.] I.
Title. II. Series: Kallen, Stuart A., 1955- Cats.
SF449.P4K35   1995
636.8'3—dc20   95-7580
                                                      CIP
                                                       AC

ABOUT THE AUTHOR
Stuart Kallen has written over 80 children's books, including many environmental science books.

Contents

LIONS, TIGERS, AND CATS

THE MIDDLE EAST

Turkey

Lebanon
Israel
Syria
Iraq
Iran (Persia)
Egypt
Jordan
Kuwait
Qatar
Saudi Arabia
United Arab Emirates
Oman
Yemen

Few animals are as beautiful and graceful as cats. And all cats are related. From the wild lions of Africa to the common house cat, all belong to the family **Felidae**. Wild cats are found almost everywhere. They include cheetahs, jaguars, lynx, ocelots, and the **domestic** cat.

People first domesticated cats around 5,000 years ago in the Middle East. Although humans have tamed them, house cats still think and act like their bigger cousins.

All cats—from cheetahs to the domestic house cat—are related.

PERSIAN CATS

Persians are probably the oldest **breed** of long-haired cats. Most other long-haired breeds are descended from Persians.

The exact origin of the Persian cat is not known. Some experts think that Persians came from Ankara, Turkey. Ankara is the birthplace of long-haired Turkish cats called **Angoras**. Persian cats look like Angoras.

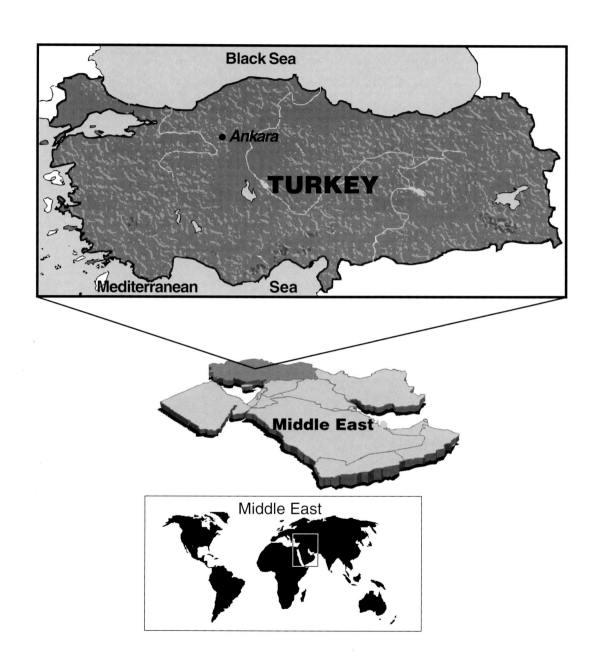

Black Sea

● *Ankara*

TURKEY

Mediterranean **Sea**

Middle East

Middle East

WHAT THEY'RE LIKE

Persian cats have a noble expression and soft, silky fur. They are clean cats and spend hours each day **grooming** their fur.

Persians make loyal pets. Sometimes they are wary of strangers. Persians can be demanding and smart, but they are not always affectionate.

Persian cats have a noble expression and soft, silky fur.

COAT AND COLOR

People favored Persians because of their unusually long, woolly coats. It is that same coat that keeps Persian owners busy with a brush.

People have **bred** Persians in nearly every color of the rainbow. A Persian's coat can be white, cream, blue, red, black, and even lilac.

People have bred Persians with other types of cats to produce **calico**, **tabby**, and **tortoise-shell** Persians. People have also bred Persians with Siamese cats to make Himalayan cats.

Persian cats come in many colors. This one is a blue-cream.

SIZE

Persians have a sturdy, round body with short, thick legs. Their faces are flat and their heads are round. Persians have pug noses and large, round eyes.

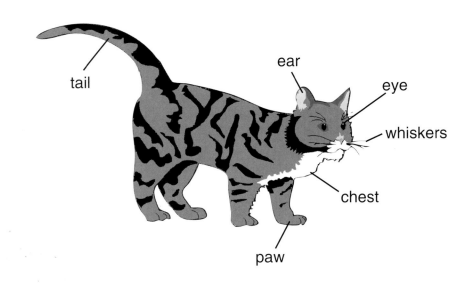

Most cats share the same features.

Notice the sturdy, thick legs and the flat, pug nose on this Persian.

CARE

The long-haired Persian needs daily brushing. This brushing takes a patient and caring owner. Without brushing, the Persian may get severe **hair balls**, which will make the cat ill.

Many people do not let their Persian outdoors because its coat can become tangled and dirty. If possible, owners should give their Persian an enclosed pen where it can enjoy the outside while staying safe and clean.

Like any pet, Persians need much love and attention. Cats make fine pets. But they still have some of their wild **instincts**.

Cats are natural hunters and do well exploring outdoors. Giving the cat a scratching post where it can sharpen its claws saves furniture from damage.

Cats bury their waste and should be trained to use a litter box. The box needs to be cleaned every day.

Persian cats need to be brushed daily.

FEEDING

Cats eat meat and fish. Hard bones that do not splinter help keep the cat's teeth and mouth clean. Water should always be available. Most cats thrive on dried cat food. Kittens enjoy their mothers milk. However, milk can cause illness in full grown cats.

Persian cats need good nutrition to maintain their thick, strong coat.

KITTENS

Female cats are **pregnant** for about 65 days. Litters range from two to eight kittens. The average cat has four kittens.

Kittens are blind and helpless for the first several weeks. Nearly three weeks later, they will start crawling and playing. At this time they may be given cat food. Nearly a month later, kittens will run, wrestle, and play games.

If the cat is a **pedigree**, it should be registered and given papers at this time. At 10 weeks the kittens are old enough to be sold or given away.

Persian kittens become playful at three to six weeks old.

BUYING A KITTEN

The best place to get a Persian cat is from a **breeder**. Cat shows are also good places to find kittens for sale.

You must decide if you want a simple pet or a show winner. A basic Persian can cost $100, with blue-ribbon winners costing as much as $1,000. When you buy a Persian, you should get **pedigree** papers that register the animal with the Cat Fanciers Association.

When buying a kitten, check it closely for signs of good health. The ears, nose, mouth, and fur should be clean. Eyes should be bright and clear. The cat should be alert and interested in its surroundings. A healthy kitten will move around with its head held high.

A Persian cat.

GLOSSARY

ANGORA (ann-GORE-uh) - A domestic cat with long, silky hair.

BREED - To raise or grow; also a group of animals that look alike and have the same type of ancestors.

CALICO - A cat that is black, red, cream, and white in color.

DOMESTICATE (doe-MESS-tih-Kate) - To tame or adapt to homelife.

FELIDAE (FEE-lih-day) - Latin name given to the cat family.

GROOMING - Cleaning and brushing.

HAIR BALLS - Balls of fur that gather in a cat's stomach after grooming it's coat by licking.

INSTINCT - A way of acting that is born in an animal, not learned.

PEDIGREE - A record of an animal's ancestors.

PREGNANT - Having one or more babies growing inside the body.

TABBY - A cat with striped fur.

TORTOISE-SHELL (TOR-tuss-shell)- A cat that is black, cream, and red in color.

Index

BIBLIOGRAPHY

Alderton, David. *Cats*. New York: Dorling Kindersley, 1992.

Clutton-Brock, Juliet. *Cat*. New York: Alfred A. Knopf, 1991.

DePrisco, Andrew. *The Mini-Atlas of Cats*. Neptune City, N.J.: T.F.H. Publications, 1991.

Taylor, David. *The Ultimate Cat Book*. New York: Simon & Schuster, 1989.